Financial Literacy 101: Managing Money With Confidence

Monica Lynne Chase

Foreword:

In a world that runs on dollars and cents, understanding how to manage your money is a superpower. Financial literacy isn't just about numbers—it's about freedom, choices, and a secure future. Whether you're just starting out or looking to sharpen your skills, this guide is designed to simplify the essentials and give you the confidence to take control of your finances. Here's to a future of smart spending, thoughtful saving, and financial independence.

TABLE OF CONTENTS

Chapter 1: Introduction to Financial Literacy

- The Importance of Financial Literacy
- Understanding Personal Finance

Chapter 2: Managing Money With Confidence

- Building a Money Management Mindset
- Overcoming Financial Anxiety

Chapter 3: Budgeting Basics

- What is a Budget?
- Types of Budgets
- Creating Your First Budget

Chapter 4: Step-by-Step Budget Templates

- Monthly Budget Template
- Annual Budget Template
- Tracking Your Expenses

Chapter 5: Understanding Credit

- What is Credit?
- The Importance of Credit Scores
- How to Check Your Credit Report

Chapter 6: Tips for Building Good Credit

- Establishing Credit
- Maintaining a Good Credit Score
- Common Credit Mistakes to Avoid

Chapter 7: Understanding Debt

- Types of Debt
- The Debt-to-Income Ratio
- How to Manage Debt Responsibly

Chapter 8: Avoiding Debt Traps

- Recognizing Warning Signs
- Strategies for Staying Out of Debt
- Seeking Help When Needed

Chapter 9: Saving for the Future

- Importance of Saving
- Setting Savings Goals
- Different Savings Accounts

Chapter 10: Beginners Guide to Investing

- What is Investing?
- Different Types of Investments
- Risk and Return

Chapter 11: Understanding Stocks, Bonds, and Mutual Funds

- Introduction to Stocks
- Introduction to Bonds
- Introduction to Mutual Funds

Chapter 12: Smart Spending

- Identifying Needs vs. Wants
- Strategies for Smart Shopping
- Making Informed Purchases

Chapter 13: Practical Tips for Financial Success

- Automating Your Finances
- Utilizing Financial Tools and Apps
- Continuous Learning in Personal Finance

Chapter 14: Conclusion

- Recap of Essential Skills
- Your Financial Journey Ahead

Chapter 1: Introduction to Financial Literacy

The Importance of Financial Literacy

Financial literacy is the foundation of effective money management and a crucial skill set for achieving economic stability and personal empowerment. In today's complex financial landscape, the ability to understand and navigate financial concepts is more important than ever. Financial literacy encompasses a range of topics, including budgeting, credit management, saving, and investing, all of which are essential for making informed decisions about one's financial future. By developing financial literacy, individuals can gain control over their finances, reduce stress, and work towards their long-term financial goals.

Understanding the basics of budgeting is one of the cornerstones of financial literacy. A well-structured budget allows individuals to track their income and expenses, ensuring they live within their means while allocating funds toward savings and investments. By mastering budgeting basics, individuals can avoid overspending, identify areas for improvement, and make informed choices about their discretionary spending. This foundational skill not only helps in managing day-to-day expenses but also prepares individuals for unexpected financial challenges, fostering resilience in the face of economic uncertainties.

Another critical aspect of financial literacy is understanding credit and debt. Knowledge of how credit works, including credit scores, interest rates, and the implications of borrowing, empowers individuals to make informed decisions about loans and credit cards. With a strong grasp of credit management, individuals can avoid common pitfalls such as accumulating high-interest debt or falling victim to predatory lending practices. Furthermore, understanding the long-term impact of debt on one's financial health enables individuals to make strategic decisions that enhance their creditworthiness and financial reputation.

Saving for the future is another vital component of financial literacy. By recognizing the importance of setting aside funds for emergencies, retirement, and specific financial goals, individuals can cultivate a savings habit that promotes financial security. This includes not only understanding the various savings options available, such as high-yield savings accounts and retirement plans, but also learning how to create a savings plan that aligns with their financial objectives. The ability to save consistently and strategically is a key driver of financial confidence and stability, allowing individuals to navigate life's uncertainties with greater assurance.

Finally, financial literacy extends to the realm of investing. For many beginners, the world of stocks, bonds, and mutual funds can seem daunting, but a solid understanding of these concepts is essential for wealth building. Financial literacy equips individuals with the knowledge to make informed investment decisions, diversify their portfolios, and understand risk versus reward. By demystifying investing, individuals can take proactive steps toward growing their wealth and securing their financial future. Ultimately, cultivating financial literacy is not just about managing money; it is about fostering a mindset of empowerment, enabling individuals to make confident, informed choices that lead to lasting financial success.

Understanding Personal Finance

Understanding personal finance is crucial for anyone looking to manage their money effectively and confidently. It encompasses various aspects of financial literacy, helping individuals make informed decisions about their income, expenses, savings, and investments. To navigate the complexities of personal finance, one must grasp key concepts such as budgeting, credit management, and the principles of saving and investing. This knowledge forms the foundation upon which sound financial practices are built, enabling individuals to achieve their financial goals while avoiding common pitfalls.

At the heart of personal finance lies budgeting, a fundamental skill that allows individuals to track their income and expenses. A well-structured budget serves as a roadmap for spending and saving, ensuring that financial resources are allocated wisely. By categorizing expenses into fixed and variable costs, individuals can identify areas where they can cut back and save more. Step-by-step budget templates can aid in this process, offering a clear framework for managing finances. Regularly reviewing and adjusting the budget ensures it remains aligned with changing financial circumstances and goals.

Understanding credit and debt is another essential component of personal finance. Credit plays a significant role in financial health, influencing everything from loan approvals to interest rates. A good credit score can open doors to favorable borrowing terms, while a poor score can lead to higher costs and limited options. It is vital to build and maintain good credit by making timely payments, keeping credit utilization low, and avoiding unnecessary debt. Practical tips for monitoring credit reports and correcting inaccuracies can empower individuals to take control of their financial standing.

Saving for the future is equally important in the realm of personal finance. Establishing an emergency fund, saving for retirement, and planning for major life expenses are critical steps toward financial security. Understanding the various savings vehicles available, such as high-yield savings accounts and certificates of deposit, can enhance one's ability to grow wealth over time. Additionally, individuals should explore investment options, including stocks, bonds, and mutual funds, to build a diversified portfolio that aligns with their risk tolerance and financial objectives.

Finally, smart spending habits can significantly impact one's overall financial well-being. Distinguishing between needs and wants, making informed purchasing decisions, and avoiding debt traps are vital strategies in this regard. Being mindful of spending not only helps individuals stay within their budget but also fosters a sense of financial discipline. By integrating these principles of personal finance, individuals can cultivate a confident approach to managing their money, ultimately leading to greater financial independence and peace of mind.

Chapter 2: Managing Money With Confidence

Building a Money Management Mindset

Building a Money Management Mindset requires a fundamental shift in how individuals perceive and interact with their finances. It begins with understanding that managing money is not merely about numbers; it is about cultivating attitudes and behaviors that promote financial well-being. Developing a growth mindset towards money involves recognizing that financial skills can be learned and improved over time. This perspective empowers individuals to take control of their financial situations, fostering confidence in their ability to make informed decisions.

The foundation of a money management mindset is self-awareness. Individuals must assess their current financial habits, attitudes, and beliefs. This introspection helps identify patterns that may hinder financial growth, such as impulsive spending or avoidance of budgeting. By acknowledging these behaviors, one can begin to implement changes that align with their financial goals. Keeping a journal of income, expenses, and emotional triggers related to spending can illuminate areas for improvement and reinforce the commitment to change.

Education plays a critical role in building a money management mindset. Familiarizing oneself with essential concepts like budgeting, credit, and investing can demystify the financial landscape. Utilizing resources such as workshops, online courses, and books can enhance financial literacy. As individuals gain knowledge, they become more equipped to navigate complex financial decisions. This understanding also enables them to discern between needs and wants, promoting smarter spending habits that align with their long-term goals.

Establishing clear financial goals is another key component of a money management mindset. Goals provide direction and motivation, serving as a roadmap for financial decisions. Whether the aim is to save for a home, pay off debt, or invest for retirement, setting specific, measurable, achievable, relevant, and time-bound (SMART) goals can guide one's financial journey. Regularly reviewing and adjusting these goals ensures they remain relevant, encouraging ongoing progress and commitment to financial well-being.

Finally, cultivating a supportive environment can reinforce a money management mindset. Surrounding oneself with like-minded individuals who prioritize financial literacy can provide encouragement and accountability. Engaging in discussions about budgeting, saving, and investing can inspire new ideas and strategies. Additionally, seeking the advice of financial professionals when needed can offer personalized guidance. By fostering a culture of financial awareness and responsibility, individuals can strengthen their money management mindset, setting the stage for a more secure financial future.

Overcoming Financial Anxiety

Financial anxiety is a common experience that can affect individuals at any stage of their financial journey. It often stems from feelings of uncertainty about money management, budgeting, or debt obligations. To overcome this anxiety, it is essential to first identify its sources. Many people feel overwhelmed by their financial situations due to a lack of understanding of basic concepts, such as credit scores, interest rates, or investment options. By recognizing these gaps in knowledge, individuals can take targeted steps to improve their financial literacy and reduce their anxiety.

One effective way to combat financial anxiety is through education. Learning fundamental concepts of managing money can empower individuals to feel more in control of their financial situations. Start by familiarizing yourself with budgeting basics, which serve as a foundation for all financial planning. Utilizing step-by-step budget templates can simplify the process of tracking income and expenses, making it less daunting. As you gain confidence in your budgeting skills, you can explore other essential topics such as understanding credit and debt, which will further enhance your financial knowledge and capabilities.

Creating a financial plan can also alleviate anxiety. A well-structured plan outlines short-term and long-term financial goals, helping you to visualize your path to financial stability. This plan could include strategies for saving for the future, paying off debt, and investing wisely. By breaking down larger goals into smaller, manageable steps, you can gradually work toward achieving them without feeling overwhelmed. Setting realistic timelines and regularly reviewing your progress can foster a sense of accomplishment that counters anxiety.

Another critical aspect of overcoming financial anxiety is developing healthy financial habits. Smart spending practices, such as distinguishing between needs and wants, can help you allocate resources more effectively. Additionally, building good credit involves consistent payment habits and understanding how credit scores work. As you cultivate these habits, you will begin to see improvement in your financial situation, reinforcing your confidence and reducing stress associated with money management.

Finally, it is important to remember that seeking support can be an invaluable part of overcoming financial anxiety. Engaging with financial advisors, joining community workshops, or even participating in online forums can provide you with necessary guidance and encouragement. Sharing experiences with others who are on similar financial journeys can help normalize feelings of anxiety and provide practical tips for navigating challenges. By building a supportive network, you can foster a more positive mindset toward your financial future and develop the resilience needed to tackle any obstacles that may arise.

Chapter 3: Budgeting Basics

What is a Budget?

A budget is a financial plan that outlines expected income and expenses over a specific period, typically monthly or yearly. It serves as a roadmap for managing finances, helping individuals and families allocate resources effectively to meet their needs and achieve financial goals. A well-structured budget not only provides clarity on where money is going but also allows for better decision-making regarding spending, saving, and investing.

The fundamental components of a budget include income, fixed expenses, variable expenses, and savings goals. Income encompasses all sources of money, such as salary, freelance work, or investments. Fixed expenses are regular, predictable payments such as rent or mortgage, utilities, and insurance. In contrast, variable expenses fluctuate, including groceries, entertainment, and discretionary spending. By categorizing these elements, individuals can gain a comprehensive view of their financial situation and identify areas where adjustments may be needed.

Creating a budget requires a systematic approach. Start by gathering financial documents that outline income and expenses, such as pay stubs, bank statements, and bills. Next, track spending patterns over a few months to understand where money is often allocated. Once this data is collected, you can draft a preliminary budget that reflects both current income and expenses. This draft serves as a baseline that can be adjusted as necessary to better align with financial objectives.

Monitoring a budget is an ongoing process that involves regular review and adjustment. Life circumstances can change—unexpected expenses may arise, or income might fluctuate—so it is crucial to revisit the budget periodically to ensure it remains relevant. This practice not only helps individuals stay on track but also enhances their ability to adapt to new financial challenges. By keeping a close eye on budget performance, individuals can take proactive steps to manage their finances effectively.

In summary, a budget is a vital tool for financial management that empowers individuals to take control of their money. It provides clarity and structure, making it easier to prioritize spending, save for future goals, and avoid debt traps. By committing to the budgeting process and making adjustments as needed, individuals can build a solid foundation for financial literacy and stability, ultimately leading to greater confidence in managing their finances.

Types of Budgets

Budgets are essential tools for managing personal finances, and understanding the different types of budgets can greatly enhance one's financial literacy. Each type of budget serves a unique purpose and can be tailored to fit individual needs and goals. By familiarizing yourself with these various budgeting methods, you can choose the one that aligns best with your financial situation and objectives, ultimately leading to more confident money management.

The first type of budget is the "zero-based budget." In this approach, every dollar earned is allocated to specific expenses, savings, or debt repayment, resulting in a balance of zero at the end of the budgeting period. This method encourages individuals to be intentional with their spending and ensures that every dollar has a purpose. By tracking all income and expenses, you can identify areas where you might cut back, helping you prioritize your financial goals, whether that's saving for a vacation, paying off debt, or investing for the future.

Another common budgeting method is the "50/30/20 budget," which divides your after-tax income into three main categories: needs, wants, and savings or debt repayment. Under this framework, 50% of your income is allocated to needs such as housing, utilities, and groceries; 30% goes toward wants, including entertainment and dining out; and the remaining 20% is dedicated to savings and debt repayment. This simple and straightforward method allows individuals to maintain a balanced approach to spending and saving, making it easier to navigate the complexities of personal finance while still enjoying life.

For those who prefer a more flexible approach, the "envelope system" might be appealing. This method involves allocating cash for specific spending categories into envelopes labeled for each category, such as groceries, entertainment, or transportation. Once the cash in an envelope is gone, no more spending occurs in that category until the next budgeting period. This tangible method can help individuals become more aware of their spending habits, encouraging mindful consumption and reducing the risk of overspending in discretionary areas.

Finally, the "line item budget" is a more detailed and structured approach, often used by organizations but equally applicable to personal finance. In this budget, expenses are categorized into specific line items, allowing for more granular tracking of where money is going. This method is particularly useful for individuals with variable income or those managing multiple financial obligations, as it provides clarity and helps ensure that all areas of spending are accounted for. By utilizing this comprehensive approach, you can gain greater insight into your financial habits, making it easier to adjust your spending and saving strategies as necessary.

Creating Your First Budget

Creating your first budget is a crucial step toward achieving financial stability and confidence. A budget serves as a roadmap for your financial journey, helping you understand where your money goes, identify your spending habits, and prioritize your financial goals. To create an effective budget, you need to gather information about your income and expenses. Start by listing all sources of income, including salaries, part-time work, and any side hustles. This will give you a clear picture of how much money you have available to allocate each month.

Next, categorize your expenses into fixed and variable costs. Fixed expenses are those that remain the same each month, such as rent or mortgage payments, insurance, and subscriptions. Variable expenses fluctuate and can include groceries, entertainment, and dining out. By understanding the difference between these two types of expenses, you can better manage your money. Make sure to track your spending for at least a month to get a realistic overview of your variable expenses. This will help you identify areas where you might be overspending or where you can cut back.

Once you have a comprehensive list of income and expenses, it's time to create the budget itself. A simple budgeting method is the 50/30/20 rule, where you allocate 50% of your income to needs, 30% to wants, and 20% to savings and debt repayment. Needs include essential expenses like housing, utilities, and groceries, while wants cover discretionary spending such as eating out and entertainment. The savings portion can be used for emergency funds, retirement accounts, or investments. Adjust these percentages according to your financial situation to create a budget that works for you.

After establishing your budget, it's crucial to monitor your spending regularly. This will help you stay accountable and make necessary adjustments if you notice that you're veering off course. Utilize budgeting tools or apps to track your expenses, making it easier to visualize your financial habits. Regular check-ins, whether weekly or monthly, can help reinforce your budgeting goals and ensure you remain on target. By being proactive and making adjustments as needed, you'll find it easier to stick to your budget over time.

Finally, remember that creating a budget is not a one-time task but an ongoing process. As your financial situation and goals evolve, so should your budget. Life changes, such as a new job, relocation, or unexpected expenses, can all impact your financial landscape. Be prepared to revisit and revise your budget periodically to reflect these changes. By establishing this habit, you'll cultivate financial literacy and develop the skills necessary to manage your money confidently, ultimately laying the groundwork for a secure financial future.

Chapter 4: Step-by-Step Budget Templates

Monthly Budget Template

A monthly budget template serves as a crucial tool for anyone looking to gain control over their finances. It provides a structured way to track income and expenses, ensuring that individuals can see where their money is going each month. The template typically includes sections for fixed expenses, variable expenses, savings, and debt repayment, allowing users to create a comprehensive overview of their financial situation. By regularly updating this template, users can monitor spending habits, identify areas for improvement, and make informed decisions about their money.

To create an effective monthly budget template, start by listing all sources of income. This may include salaries, bonuses, freelance work, or any other form of revenue. It is essential to calculate the total income accurately, as this figure will serve as the foundation for the entire budget. Once income is established, the next step is to categorize expenses into fixed and variable costs. Fixed expenses, such as rent or mortgage payments, utility bills, and insurance, remain consistent each month, while variable expenses, like groceries, entertainment, and dining out, can fluctuate. Understanding these categories helps individuals see where adjustments can be made.

After categorizing expenses, it is beneficial to allocate a portion of the budget to savings and debt repayment. A vital component of financial health is saving for emergencies and future goals. Setting aside at least 20% of income for savings is a common recommendation, but individuals should adjust this percentage based on their unique situations. Additionally, if there are existing debts, a systematic approach to repayment should be included in the budget. This could involve allocating funds toward high-interest debts first or following the snowball method, where smaller debts are paid off first to build momentum.

Once the template is filled out, it is important to regularly review and adjust it as necessary. Life circumstances can change, impacting income and expenses in various ways. Monthly check-ins allow individuals to stay accountable and make necessary changes to their spending or savings plans. This practice not only helps in adhering to the budget but also fosters a habit of financial mindfulness. By consistently using the budget template, individuals can develop a clearer picture of their financial journey and make strides toward achieving their financial goals.

Lastly, using a monthly budget template can lead to improved financial literacy and confidence. It demystifies the budgeting process and encourages individuals to take an active role in managing their finances. As they gain experience and see the benefits of sticking to a budget—such as reduced stress, increased savings, and a better understanding of credit and debt—they will be more likely to engage in other essential financial practices. The journey to financial literacy may begin with a simple budget template, but the skills and confidence gained from this practice can have lasting effects on one's overall financial well-being.

Annual Budget Template

An annual budget template serves as a guiding framework for individuals seeking to take control of their financial situation. It allows for a comprehensive overview of anticipated income and expenditures over the course of a year, helping you to plan for both expected and unexpected financial events. By laying out your financial landscape, this template enables you to identify areas where you can save, allocate funds for investments, and ensure you are living within your means. This structured approach not only enhances financial literacy but also promotes a sense of confidence in managing your money.

To create an effective annual budget template, begin by listing all sources of income. This includes your salary, any side hustles, investment returns, and any other streams of revenue. Once you have an accurate picture of your total income, you can move forward to catalog your anticipated expenses. Categorize these expenses into fixed costs, such as rent or mortgage payments, and variable costs, including groceries, entertainment, and discretionary spending. This clear distinction will help you identify which expenses are necessary and which can be adjusted or eliminated, fostering smarter spending habits.

After establishing your income and expenses, the next step is to project any potential changes throughout the year. Consider factors such as seasonal expenses, upcoming life events like weddings or vacations, and potential income fluctuations. This foresight is crucial in budgeting, as it prepares you for unforeseen circumstances and helps mitigate the risk of falling into debt. By accounting for these variations, you can build a more resilient budget that allows for flexibility without compromising your financial goals.

Additionally, it's essential to incorporate a savings plan into your annual budget template. Allocate specific amounts for emergency savings, retirement contributions, and short-term savings goals. A well-rounded budget not only focuses on current expenses but also prioritizes future financial security. By setting aside a portion of your income for savings each month, you cultivate a habit of saving that can lead to greater financial freedom and peace of mind.

Finally, regularly review and adjust your annual budget. Life circumstances change, and so should your financial plans. By revisiting your budget on a quarterly basis, you can assess your progress, identify areas for improvement, and make necessary adjustments to ensure you are on track to meet your financial goals. This practice reinforces the importance of financial literacy and empowers you to manage your money with confidence, paving the way for a secure financial future.

Tracking Your Expenses

Tracking your expenses is a fundamental practice in managing your finances effectively. It involves recording and categorizing every dollar you spend, which provides you with valuable insights into your spending habits. By diligently tracking your expenses, you can identify areas where you may be overspending, allowing you to make informed decisions about where to cut back. This practice not only aids in creating a realistic budget but also establishes a foundation for achieving your financial goals.

To begin tracking your expenses, consider using a method that suits your lifestyle and preferences. This could be as simple as maintaining a handwritten ledger, utilizing a spreadsheet, or employing personal finance software and mobile applications designed for expense tracking. Whichever method you choose, consistency is key. Make it a habit to record every transaction, no matter how small, to ensure you have a complete picture of your financial situation. This level of detail can help you uncover patterns in your spending that you may not have noticed before.

Once you have established a routine for tracking your expenses, categorize them into meaningful groups such as housing, transportation, groceries, entertainment, and savings. Creating these categories enables you to see where your money is going and how much of your income is allocated to each area. This categorization also facilitates the comparison of your actual spending against your budgeted amounts, helping to highlight discrepancies that may require adjustments. Regularly reviewing these categories can provide motivation to stick to your budget and make more mindful spending choices.

In addition to enhancing your budgeting efforts, tracking your expenses can play a crucial role in building and maintaining good credit. When you are aware of your spending patterns, you can better manage your credit utilization ratio, which is a significant factor in your credit score. Keeping your credit card balances low and making timely payments becomes much easier when you have a clear understanding of your financial habits. This proactive approach can lead to improved creditworthiness, paving the way for better borrowing opportunities in the future.

Finally, tracking your expenses is not merely about keeping your finances in check; it is also about fostering a mindset of financial responsibility and awareness. By regularly engaging with your financial data, you develop a deeper understanding of your economic behaviors and priorities. This awareness empowers you to make informed decisions, whether you are saving for a major purchase, planning for retirement, or investing in your future. Ultimately, mastering the art of expense tracking equips you with essential skills that will serve you throughout your financial journey, instilling confidence in your ability to manage money effectively.

Chapter 5: Understanding Credit

What is Credit?

Credit is a fundamental concept in personal finance that refers to the ability to borrow money or access goods and services with the understanding that payment will be made in the future. It plays a crucial role in most financial transactions, influencing everything from purchasing a home to securing a loan for education or starting a business. At its core, credit represents a relationship of trust between lenders and borrowers. Lenders provide resources with the expectation that borrowers will repay the amount borrowed, often with interest, over a specified period.

The evaluation of creditworthiness is often determined through a credit score, which is a numerical representation of a person's credit history and financial behavior. Credit scores range from poor to excellent, and they are influenced by several factors, including payment history, credit utilization, length of credit history, types of credit accounts, and recent credit inquiries. Understanding how these elements affect credit scores is essential for individuals striving to manage their finances effectively. A higher credit score generally leads to better borrowing terms, such as lower interest rates and more favorable loan conditions.

Credit can be classified into two main types: revolving credit and installment credit. Revolving credit, such as credit cards, allows borrowers to access a line of credit up to a certain limit, giving them the flexibility to borrow and repay repeatedly. On the other hand, installment credit involves borrowing a fixed amount of money that is repaid in regular installments over time, such as in the case of a mortgage or auto loan. Recognizing the differences between these types of credit is vital for effective money management, as it influences spending habits and financial planning.

Responsible use of credit can lead to numerous benefits, including the ability to build a solid credit history, which is essential for major purchases like homes and cars. Good credit management can also provide access to lower insurance premiums and job opportunities, as some employers consider credit history during the hiring process. However, misusing credit can result in significant financial challenges, such as accumulating debt that can lead to bankruptcy or foreclosure. Therefore, it is critical to approach credit with a clear understanding of its implications and to develop strategies for maintaining a healthy credit profile.

In conclusion, credit is not just a financial tool; it is an integral part of navigating the broader financial landscape. By understanding what credit is and how it works, individuals can make informed decisions that positively impact their financial well-being. This knowledge empowers people to leverage credit wisely, avoid common pitfalls, and ultimately achieve their financial goals. As we delve deeper into the intricacies of credit and debt in this book, you will gain practical insights and tips that will enhance your ability to manage money confidently and effectively.

The Importance of Credit Scores

Credit scores play a crucial role in personal finance and can significantly influence an individual's financial opportunities. A credit score is a numerical representation of a person's creditworthiness, reflecting their ability to repay borrowed money. Ranging from 300 to 850, this score is determined by various factors, including payment history, credit utilization, length of credit history, types of credit accounts, and recent inquiries. Understanding the importance of credit scores is essential for anyone looking to manage their money effectively, as it can impact everything from loan approval to interest rates on credit cards and mortgages.

One of the primary reasons credit scores are important is their direct effect on borrowing costs. Lenders use credit scores to assess the risk associated with lending money. A higher score typically results in lower interest rates, which can save individuals thousands of dollars over the life of a loan. For example, a person with a score of 750 may secure a mortgage at a significantly lower rate than someone with a score of 620. This difference can lead to substantial savings in monthly payments and overall loan costs, making it clear that maintaining a good credit score is a financial advantage.

Moreover, credit scores can affect non-loan-related aspects of life, such as renting an apartment, securing insurance, or even getting a job. Many landlords check potential tenants' credit scores as part of the application process to gauge their financial responsibility. Similarly, insurance companies may use credit scores to determine premiums for policies. Some employers also consider credit history during the hiring process, particularly for positions that involve financial responsibilities. Thus, a good credit score can open doors and provide individuals with a range of opportunities that may otherwise be unavailable.

Building and maintaining a strong credit score requires a proactive approach. Key strategies include making timely payments, keeping credit utilization low, and regularly reviewing credit reports for errors. Individuals should aim to pay their bills on time and in full, as late payments can significantly hurt their scores. Additionally, keeping credit card balances below 30% of the available credit limit is advisable, as high utilization can signal financial distress to lenders. Regularly monitoring credit reports allows individuals to catch and dispute inaccuracies, ensuring their credit score accurately reflects their financial behavior.

In conclusion, understanding and prioritizing credit scores is an essential skill for effective money management. A strong credit score can lead to lower borrowing costs, better rental opportunities, and even career advancements. By adopting responsible credit practices and remaining informed about their financial standing, individuals can enhance their credit profiles and position themselves for long-term financial success. Emphasizing the importance of credit scores is a vital step in building a solid financial foundation and achieving greater confidence in managing personal finances.

How to Check Your Credit Report

Checking your credit report is an essential step in managing your financial health. Your credit report reflects your credit history and is used by lenders to determine your creditworthiness. This report includes information about your credit accounts, payment history, outstanding debts, and any public records such as bankruptcies or tax liens. Understanding how to check your credit report not only empowers you to monitor your financial standing but also helps you identify errors or fraudulent activity that could harm your credit score.

To begin, you are entitled to one free credit report per year from each of the three major credit reporting agencies: Equifax, Experian, and TransUnion. You can obtain your free reports at AnnualCreditReport.com, the only federally authorized source for free credit reports. When you visit this website, you will need to provide some personal information, such as your name, Social Security number, and address, to verify your identity. It is advisable to stagger your requests throughout the year, so you can monitor your credit more frequently without incurring costs.

Once you have accessed your credit report, take the time to review it thoroughly. Look for any discrepancies, such as accounts that do not belong to you or payment histories that are inaccurately reported. Pay close attention to the dates of account openings and payment patterns, as these elements significantly impact your credit score. If you find any errors, you can dispute them directly with the credit reporting agency. This process typically involves submitting a formal dispute along with any supporting documentation that proves the inaccuracies.

In addition to checking for errors, it is important to understand the various components of your credit report. The report is generally divided into sections, including personal information, credit accounts, inquiries, and public records. Familiarize yourself with how each section contributes to your overall credit score. For example, your payment history makes up a significant portion of your score, so it's crucial to ensure that your payments are reported accurately. Understanding these components can help you prioritize which areas to focus on for improvement.

Finally, regularly checking your credit report is a proactive way to maintain financial health and improve your credit score over time. By staying informed about your credit standing, you position yourself to make better financial decisions, whether that means obtaining favorable loan terms or understanding the impact of your credit on future investments. Taking these steps not only builds confidence in managing your finances but also equips you with the knowledge to navigate the complexities of credit and debt responsibly.

Chapter 6: Tips for Building Good Credit

Establishing Credit

Establishing credit is a fundamental step in building a solid financial foundation. Credit is not just a tool for borrowing; it plays a significant role in determining your financial health and opportunities. A good credit score can influence your ability to secure loans, obtain favorable interest rates, and even rent an apartment. Understanding how credit works, and actively working to establish and maintain it, is crucial for anyone looking to manage their finances effectively.

To begin establishing credit, you must first understand the various types of credit available. The most common forms include credit cards, personal loans, student loans, and auto loans. Each type of credit can contribute to your overall credit history and score, but they also come with different responsibilities. For beginners, starting with a secured credit card is often recommended. This type of card requires a cash deposit, which serves as your credit limit. It allows you to build credit while minimizing the risk for lenders, making it an accessible option for those new to credit.

Once you have a credit account, it is essential to manage it wisely. Responsible credit usage entails making timely payments and keeping your credit utilization ratio low. A good rule of thumb is to use no more than 30% of your available credit. This demonstrates to lenders that you can handle credit responsibly without overextending yourself. Additionally, establishing a payment schedule can help ensure that you never miss a due date, as timely payments are one of the most significant factors in determining your credit score.

Building a positive credit history takes time and patience. Regularly monitoring your credit report is a crucial part of this process. You are entitled to one free credit report per year from each of the major credit bureaus. Reviewing these reports can help you identify areas for improvement, catch errors, and understand how your credit activity affects your score. If you notice any discrepancies, it is important to dispute them promptly to maintain an accurate credit history.

Finally, as you establish credit, remember that it is just one aspect of your overall financial journey. While building good credit can open doors, it is also essential to develop healthy financial habits. This includes budgeting, saving for emergencies, and investing for the future. By combining a strong credit profile with sound financial practices, you can achieve greater financial stability and confidence, ultimately leading to a more secure and prosperous future.

Maintaining a Good Credit Score

Maintaining a good credit score is a fundamental aspect of financial literacy that can significantly influence your ability to secure loans, obtain favorable interest rates, and even affect job prospects in certain fields. A credit score typically ranges from 300 to 850, with higher scores indicating better creditworthiness. Understanding what factors contribute to your credit score is crucial. These include payment history, amounts owed, length of credit history, types of credit used, and new credit inquiries. By grasping these components, you can take proactive steps to ensure that your score remains healthy.

One of the most effective ways to maintain a good credit score is to consistently make timely payments on all your debts. Payment history accounts for a significant portion of your credit score, making it essential to prioritize due dates and avoid late payments. Setting up automatic payments or reminders can help you stay on track. Additionally, if you are struggling to meet payments, it is advisable to communicate with creditors to explore potential solutions, such as payment plans or deferments, rather than missing payments altogether.

Another critical factor in maintaining a good credit score is managing your credit utilization ratio, which is the percentage of your available credit that you are currently using. Ideally, this ratio should be kept below 30%. To achieve this, consider paying down existing debt and avoiding maxing out credit cards. If possible, request a credit limit increase on your existing accounts, as this can help lower your utilization ratio without increasing your spending. Regularly reviewing your credit report will also allow you to monitor your utilization and make necessary adjustments.

Establishing a diverse mix of credit types can further bolster your credit score. Lenders typically view a variety of credit accounts, such as credit cards, installment loans, and retail accounts, as a positive indicator of your ability to manage different types of debt responsibly. However, it is essential to approach this strategy with caution; opening new credit accounts should be done judiciously to avoid unnecessary inquiries that can temporarily lower your score. Instead, focus on maintaining older accounts, as a longer credit history generally benefits your score.

Finally, staying informed about your credit score and credit report is vital for effective management. Regularly checking your credit report for errors allows you to dispute inaccuracies that could negatively impact your score. Many financial institutions and credit monitoring services offer free access to your credit report. By reviewing this information, you can identify patterns, understand your financial behavior, and make informed decisions about your credit use. Armed with this knowledge, you can take concrete steps to maintain and improve your credit score, ensuring that you are well-prepared for future financial opportunities.

Common Credit Mistakes to Avoid

One of the most significant pitfalls individuals encounter in managing their credit is failing to monitor their credit reports regularly. Credit reports contain crucial information about your credit history, including your payment habits, outstanding debts, and credit inquiries. Neglecting to check your reports can lead to missing errors or fraudulent activity that can harm your credit score. It is essential to review your reports at least annually, which you can do for free through various resources. Staying informed about your credit status allows you to address any issues promptly and maintain a healthy credit profile.

Another common mistake is accumulating excessive debt without a clear plan for repayment. Many individuals get caught up in the convenience of credit cards and loans, often leading to a cycle of debt that can be challenging to escape. It's crucial to establish a budget that includes not only your monthly expenses but also a strategy for paying down any outstanding debts. By prioritizing debt repayment within your budget, you can avoid falling into a trap where interest accrues faster than you can pay it down, ultimately damaging your credit score.

In addition to monitoring credit reports and managing debt, many individuals misunderstand the importance of credit utilization. Credit utilization refers to the ratio of your current credit card balances to your credit limits. A common mistake is using a large portion of your available credit, which can negatively impact your credit score. Keeping your utilization below 30 percent is generally recommended. By managing your credit card usage wisely and paying off balances regularly, you can enhance your credit profile and demonstrate responsible credit behavior.

Moreover, applying for multiple credit accounts within a short timeframe can signal financial instability to lenders. Each time you apply for credit, a hard inquiry is made on your report, which can lower your credit score temporarily. Individuals often make the mistake of shopping around for the best credit card or loan rates without realizing that multiple applications can have a cumulative negative effect. To avoid this, it's advisable to do thorough research and limit your applications to those that are absolutely necessary. This strategy will help maintain a stable credit score while allowing you to make informed financial decisions.

Lastly, many people overlook the impact of timely payments on their credit scores. Late payments can significantly damage your creditworthiness and remain on your report for up to seven years. A common mistake is assuming that missing one or two payments won't matter. To avoid this, set up reminders or automatic payments to ensure that you meet your financial obligations on time. By prioritizing punctuality in your payments, you not only protect your credit score but also cultivate a responsible financial habit that will benefit you in the long run.

Chapter 7: Understanding Debt

Types of Debt

Debt comes in various forms, each serving different purposes and carrying distinct implications for your financial health. Understanding the types of debt is crucial for managing your finances effectively. The two primary categories of debt are secured and unsecured debt. Secured debt is backed by collateral, meaning that if you fail to repay it, the lender can claim the asset used as security. A common example of secured debt is a mortgage, where the property itself serves as collateral. In contrast, unsecured debt does not involve collateral, making it riskier for lenders. Credit cards and personal loans fall into this category, often resulting in higher interest rates due to the lack of security.

Within these broad categories, debt can further be classified as revolving or installment debt. Revolving debt, typically associated with credit cards, allows you to borrow up to a certain limit and pay it back over time, with the flexibility to borrow again as you repay. This type of debt can be convenient, but it can also lead to overspending and accumulating high interest if not managed carefully. Installment debt, on the other hand, is borrowed in a lump sum and repaid in fixed amounts over a set period. Examples include car loans and student loans. Understanding these distinctions will help you make informed decisions about borrowing and repayment.

Another important classification of debt is consumer debt versus business debt. Consumer debt refers to personal loans taken out for personal consumption, such as home improvements, vacations, or medical expenses. This type of debt can strain your budget if not managed wisely, as it often comes with higher interest rates. Business debt is incurred by businesses to finance operations, investments, or expansion. While this type of debt can be beneficial for growth, it also carries risks, particularly if the business does not generate enough revenue to cover repayments.

In addition to these classifications, understanding the terms of each type of debt is vital. Interest rates, repayment periods, and fees can differ significantly between types of debt. For instance, student loans often come with lower interest rates and deferred payment options, while credit card debt can accumulate interest rapidly. Familiarizing yourself with these terms can empower you to negotiate better deals and choose the right type of debt for your financial situation.

Finally, awareness of good debt versus bad debt can guide you in making strategic financial choices. Good debt is often considered an investment that can appreciate over time, such as a mortgage or certain student loans that lead to higher earning potential. Bad debt typically refers to high-interest borrowing that does not contribute to your long-term financial goals, like excessive credit card debt for consumer goods. By assessing the types of debt you encounter and their potential impact on your financial well-being, you can make more informed choices, ultimately leading to a healthier financial future.

The Debt-to-Income Ratio

The debt-to-income (DTI) ratio is a crucial metric in personal finance that helps individuals understand their financial health, especially when it comes to borrowing. This ratio compares an individual's total monthly debt payments to their gross monthly income, expressed as a percentage. Lenders often use the DTI ratio to assess a borrower's ability to manage monthly payments and repay debts. A lower DTI ratio indicates a healthier financial situation, suggesting that a smaller portion of income goes towards debt repayment, allowing for more disposable income for savings, investments, and other expenses.

To calculate your DTI ratio, start by adding up all your monthly debt obligations. This includes payments on mortgages, car loans, student loans, credit cards, and any other recurring debt. Once you have this total, divide it by your gross monthly income, which is your income before taxes and other deductions. For example, if your total monthly debts amount to $2,000 and your gross monthly income is $6,000, your DTI ratio would be approximately 33%. Most financial experts recommend keeping your DTI ratio below 36%, as higher ratios can indicate potential financial distress and may limit your borrowing capacity.

Understanding your DTI ratio is essential not only for securing loans but also for managing your overall financial strategy. If your DTI is higher than recommended, it may signal the need to reassess your spending habits and debt levels. This could involve creating a budget that prioritizes debt repayment, seeking to reduce unnecessary expenses, or exploring options for increasing your income. By improving your DTI ratio, you position yourself more favorably in the eyes of lenders, which can lead to better interest rates and loan terms.

Moreover, maintaining a healthy DTI ratio is a long-term financial goal that contributes to financial stability. As you work towards reducing your debt, consider implementing a proactive approach to credit management. This includes making timely payments, avoiding new debt accumulation, and utilizing credit responsibly. Such practices not only help in lowering your DTI but also build your credit history, which is another critical aspect of financial health. A strong credit score can enhance your ability to secure loans with favorable terms, further supporting your financial objectives.

In conclusion, the debt-to-income ratio serves as a vital tool in personal finance management. By understanding and actively managing your DTI, you empower yourself to make informed financial decisions that promote stability and growth. Regularly monitoring this ratio can help you stay on track with your financial goals, ensuring that you remain within a healthy range that allows for both debt repayment and the pursuit of other financial aspirations, such as saving and investing for the future.

How to Manage Debt Responsibly

Managing debt responsibly is a critical skill that every individual must develop to maintain financial stability and ensure long-term well-being. The first step in this process involves understanding the types of debt one may encounter. Debt can be categorized into two main types: secured and unsecured. Secured debt, such as mortgages and auto loans, is backed by collateral, while unsecured debt, which includes credit card balances and personal loans, is not. Recognizing the differences between these types of debt helps individuals make informed decisions about borrowing and repayment.

Once the types of debt are understood, it is essential to establish a clear strategy for managing it. This begins with creating a comprehensive budget that outlines income and expenses. By tracking spending habits, individuals can identify areas where they can cut back and allocate more funds towards debt repayment. A well-structured budget not only aids in managing current debt but also acts as a preventive measure against future financial pitfalls. Utilizing step-by-step budget templates can simplify this process and provide a clear roadmap for financial health.

Another important aspect of responsible debt management is prioritizing debt repayment. Individuals should focus on paying off high-interest debts first, as these can accumulate quickly and lead to greater financial strain. The snowball and avalanche methods are two popular strategies for tackling debt. The snowball method involves paying off the smallest debts first to gain momentum, while the avalanche method targets debts with the highest interest rates. Whichever method is chosen, consistency in payments and a commitment to reducing debt over time are crucial.

Maintaining good credit is also vital in managing debt responsibly. A strong credit score can lead to better interest rates on loans and credit cards, making it easier to manage existing debt. Individuals should regularly review their credit reports to ensure accuracy and address any discrepancies promptly. Additionally, paying bills on time, keeping credit utilization low, and avoiding unnecessary credit inquiries are essential practices for building and maintaining good credit. These habits not only support responsible debt management but also contribute to overall financial health.

Finally, individuals need to prepare for unexpected financial challenges by building an emergency fund. Having savings set aside can prevent the need to rely on credit in times of crisis, which can lead to increased debt. Aim to save at least three to six months' worth of living expenses to create a financial cushion. This proactive approach not only fosters financial security but also reinforces responsible debt management practices. By understanding debt, creating a budget, prioritizing repayments, maintaining good credit, and preparing for emergencies, individuals can navigate their financial journeys with confidence and resilience.

Chapter 8: Avoiding Debt Traps

Recognizing Warning Signs

Recognizing warning signs in your financial life is crucial for maintaining control over your economic well-being. Many individuals navigate their financial journeys without fully understanding the subtle indicators that suggest they may be heading toward trouble. These signs can manifest in various forms, from changes in spending habits to increased reliance on credit. By familiarizing yourself with these warning signs, you can take proactive measures to address issues before they escalate, ensuring that you remain on a path to financial stability.

One common warning sign is the consistent use of credit cards to cover everyday expenses. If you find yourself regularly charging groceries or bills instead of using cash or debit, it may indicate that your budget is not aligned with your income. This habit can lead to a cycle of debt that becomes increasingly difficult to break. Keeping a close eye on your spending patterns is essential; if credit card usage becomes a necessity rather than a convenience, it's time to reassess your financial plan and make adjustments to your budget.

Another red flag is the accumulation of bills or notices from creditors. If you are avoiding opening your mail because of anxiety about unpaid debts, this is a strong indicator that you are not managing your finances effectively. Ignoring these communications can lead to late fees, increased interest rates, and damage to your credit score. Establishing a routine for reviewing your financial obligations and addressing them promptly can help you regain control and reduce stress related to outstanding debts.

Additionally, a sudden increase in your financial stress levels can signal that something is amiss. If you find yourself frequently worrying about money or feeling overwhelmed by financial decisions, it may be time to take a step back and evaluate your financial situation. Stress can often cloud judgment, leading to poor financial choices. Consider seeking advice from a financial professional or utilizing resources that focus on financial literacy to help you navigate your concerns and develop a clearer plan for the future.

Lastly, a lack of savings can be a significant warning sign. If you do not have an emergency fund or are unable to set aside money for future goals, you may be living beyond your means. Establishing a savings plan, even if it starts with a small amount, can help create a buffer against unexpected expenses and provide peace of mind. Understanding the importance of saving and making it a priority in your budgeting process is vital for long-term financial health. By being aware of these warning signs and taking action, you can foster a more confident and secure financial future.

Strategies for Staying Out of Debt

One of the most effective strategies for staying out of debt is developing a comprehensive budget. A budget serves as a financial roadmap, outlining your income and expenses. Begin by tracking your spending habits for a month to identify areas where you can cut back. Categorize your expenses into fixed (like rent and utilities) and variable (such as dining out and entertainment). By establishing a clear budget, you can allocate funds toward essential needs while limiting discretionary spending. This disciplined approach not only helps prevent overspending but also fosters a greater awareness of your financial situation.

Another key strategy is building an emergency fund. Life is unpredictable, and unexpected expenses can lead to reliance on credit cards or loans, pushing you into debt. Aim to save at least three to six months' worth of living expenses in a separate, easily accessible account. This fund serves as a safety net during financial emergencies, such as medical bills or car repairs, allowing you to manage these situations without resorting to borrowing. Regularly contributing to your emergency fund, even if it's a small amount, will create a sense of financial security and reduce the likelihood of debt accumulation.

Educating yourself about credit and its implications is crucial for staying out of debt. Understanding how credit scores work and what factors contribute to them can empower you to make informed decisions about borrowing. Regularly check your credit report for inaccuracies and ensure you are aware of your credit utilization ratio. Keeping this ratio below 30 percent is advisable, as it demonstrates responsible credit management. By maintaining good credit, you can secure lower interest rates on loans when necessary, preventing the high costs associated with poor credit.

Practicing smart spending habits can significantly reduce the risk of falling into debt. Before making a purchase, implement the 24-hour rule; wait a day to evaluate whether the item is a need or a want. Additionally, consider using cash for discretionary purchases to limit spending, as it's easier to overspend with credit cards. Take advantage of sales and discounts, but ensure that these opportunities align with your budget and needs. By being mindful of your spending behaviors, you can maintain control over your finances and avoid unnecessary debt.

Lastly, setting financial goals can provide motivation to stay on track and out of debt. Whether you aim to save for a vacation, pay off a specific bill, or invest in your education, having clear objectives can guide your financial decisions. Break larger goals into smaller, manageable steps and celebrate your achievements along the way. This not only enhances your financial literacy but also builds confidence in your ability to manage money effectively. By focusing on your goals, you create a positive mindset towards financial management, making it less likely for debt to become a part of your journey.

Seeking Help When Needed

Seeking help when needed is a critical aspect of effective financial management. Many individuals may feel overwhelmed by their financial situations, whether it involves budgeting, understanding credit, or navigating the complexities of investments. The first step in seeking assistance is recognizing that it is not a sign of weakness but a proactive approach to enhancing one's financial literacy. Engaging with resources such as financial advisors, community programs, or online platforms can provide valuable insights and guidance tailored to one's unique financial circumstances.

One of the most common areas where individuals seek help is in budgeting. Creating a budget can seem daunting, especially for those just starting their financial journey. Utilizing step-by-step budget templates can simplify this process, but sometimes, additional support is necessary. Financial workshops, both in-person and virtual, often offer practical tips and strategies for building a budget that aligns with personal goals. These workshops can also foster a sense of community, allowing participants to share experiences and learn from one another.

Understanding credit and debt is another area where seeking help can be beneficial. Many people struggle with managing their credit scores or understanding how interest rates affect their debt. Consulting with a credit counselor can provide clarity on how to improve credit scores and develop a plan to pay down debts effectively. This professional guidance can help demystify the components of credit reports and empower individuals to make informed decisions that enhance their financial standing.

Saving for the future can also pose challenges, particularly for those unfamiliar with investment options. Seeking help from financial advisors can illuminate the various avenues available, such as stocks, bonds, and mutual funds. These professionals can explain investment strategies in beginner-friendly terms, helping individuals understand risk and return while also considering their long-term financial goals. Additionally, there are many online resources and tools that can assist in making informed investment choices.

Finally, avoiding debt traps is crucial for maintaining financial health. Many individuals may not recognize the signs of falling into debt or the impact of high-interest loans. Educational resources, such as financial literacy courses, can equip individuals with the skills necessary to identify and avoid these pitfalls. By seeking help and engaging with educational materials, individuals can gain the confidence needed to manage their money effectively and make sound financial decisions that lead to a more secure future.

Chapter 9: Saving for the Future

Importance of Saving

Saving money is a fundamental aspect of financial literacy that serves as the foundation for achieving long-term financial stability and independence. By developing a consistent saving habit, individuals can create a safety net that protects against unforeseen expenses and emergencies. This financial cushion not only alleviates stress during challenging times but also empowers individuals to make informed decisions about their future. Saving is not merely a practice; it is a mindset that fosters responsibility and foresight, essential skills for anyone navigating the complexities of personal finance.

One of the primary reasons saving is essential is that it provides security and peace of mind. Life is unpredictable, and unexpected expenses such as medical emergencies, car repairs, or job loss can arise at any moment. Having savings set aside enables individuals to handle these situations without resorting to credit cards or loans, which can lead to debt traps. By prioritizing savings, individuals can maintain control over their finances and avoid the burden of high-interest debts that can accumulate quickly and become overwhelming.

In addition to providing a safety net, saving money lays the groundwork for future financial goals. Whether it's purchasing a home, funding education, or planning for retirement, having a savings plan is crucial. Setting specific savings goals allows individuals to create a roadmap for their financial future and encourages disciplined spending habits. By breaking down larger goals into manageable savings targets, individuals can remain motivated and track their progress, ultimately leading to greater financial achievement and confidence.

Furthermore, saving money opens up opportunities for investing. Once individuals have established a solid savings base, they can explore various investment options such as stocks, bonds, and mutual funds. Investing is a powerful tool for building wealth over time, but it requires a certain level of financial security to take on the associated risks. By prioritizing saving, individuals can ensure they have the capital needed to invest in their future, further enhancing their financial literacy and understanding of how to grow their wealth effectively.

Lastly, fostering a culture of saving contributes to overall financial health. It encourages individuals to adopt mindful spending habits and make informed financial decisions, which are critical components of managing money effectively. By embracing saving as a lifelong habit, individuals not only prepare for their personal financial goals but also set an example for their families and communities. This ripple effect can lead to a more financially literate society where individuals feel empowered to manage their resources wisely and confidently.

Setting Savings Goals

Setting savings goals is a fundamental component of personal finance that can significantly enhance your ability to manage money effectively. Savings goals provide direction and motivation, allowing you to prioritize your financial objectives and allocate resources accordingly. Whether you are saving for short-term needs, such as an emergency fund or a vacation, or long-term aspirations, like a home purchase or retirement, having clear goals helps you stay focused and disciplined in your financial journey.

To establish effective savings goals, it is essential to follow the SMART criteria: Specific, Measurable, Achievable, Relevant, and Time-bound. Specificity ensures that your goals are clear and well-defined. For example, instead of saying, "I want to save money," you could specify, "I want to save $5,000 for a down payment on a car." Measurable goals allow you to track your progress, while achievable goals should be realistic based on your income and expenses. Ensuring that your goals are relevant to your life and financial situation helps maintain motivation, and setting a timeline creates urgency, prompting you to take action.

Once you have established your savings goals, the next step is to create a savings plan that aligns with those objectives. This plan should include how much you need to save each month and the strategies you will employ to reach your goals. Consider automating your savings by setting up a direct transfer from your checking account to a savings account. This method simplifies the process and ensures that you consistently contribute to your savings without needing to think about it. Additionally, review your budget to identify areas where you can cut back on spending to increase your savings potential.

Regularly reviewing and adjusting your savings goals is crucial as life circumstances and financial situations can change. It's important to stay flexible and be willing to reassess your goals periodically. This might involve increasing your savings target if your income rises or adjusting your timeline if unexpected expenses arise. By staying engaged with your savings plan, you can maintain a proactive approach to managing your finances and adapt to shifting priorities.

Finally, celebrate your achievements along the way, no matter how small. Reaching savings milestones can boost your confidence and reinforce positive financial habits. Whether it's treating yourself to a small reward or simply acknowledging your progress, taking time to recognize your efforts can motivate you to continue on your path toward financial security. Setting and achieving savings goals not only prepares you for future expenses but also fosters a sense of accomplishment and control over your financial life.

Different Savings Accounts

Different savings accounts serve various purposes and are designed to help individuals achieve specific financial goals. Understanding the types of savings accounts available is crucial for effective money management. Each account type offers unique features, benefits, and interest rates, making it important to select the right one based on your financial objectives. In this section, we will explore the most common types of savings accounts, highlighting their key characteristics and how they can fit into your overall financial strategy.

Regular savings accounts are typically offered by banks and credit unions, providing easy access to funds while earning a modest interest rate. These accounts are ideal for short-term savings goals or for building an emergency fund. The liquidity of regular savings accounts allows account holders to withdraw money without penalties, making them a convenient option for those who may need quick access to cash. However, the interest rates on these accounts are generally lower than other savings vehicles, which may not significantly grow your savings over time.

High-yield savings accounts are another option that many individuals consider. These accounts, often provided by online banks, offer higher interest rates compared to traditional savings accounts. The increased interest can help your savings grow faster, making it a suitable choice for those looking to maximize their earnings on short- to medium-term savings. While these accounts may have some restrictions, such as limited withdrawals per month, they provide a balance between earning potential and accessibility, making them attractive for those who prioritize both growth and flexibility.

Certificates of Deposit (CDs) represent a more structured savings option. When you invest in a CD, you agree to leave your money deposited for a fixed term, which can range from a few months to several years. In return, you receive a higher interest rate than that offered by regular savings accounts. However, accessing funds before the maturity date typically incurs penalties, which can discourage impulsive withdrawals. CDs are an excellent choice for individuals who have specific savings goals and can commit their funds for an extended period, as they provide predictable growth and security.

Money market accounts combine features of both savings and checking accounts, often offering higher interest rates and limited check-writing capabilities. These accounts can be appealing for those who want to earn more on their savings while retaining some level of liquidity. However, money market accounts may require a higher minimum balance to open and maintain, which could be a consideration for individuals just starting their savings journey. By understanding the different types of savings accounts available, you can make informed decisions that align with your financial goals, helping you manage your money more effectively and confidently.

Chapter 10: Beginners Guide to Investing

What is Investing?

Investing is the act of allocating resources, typically money, with the expectation of generating an income or profit. It is a fundamental aspect of personal finance and plays a crucial role in wealth accumulation and financial security. At its core, investing involves making informed decisions about where to put your money to work for you rather than simply letting it sit idle. This proactive approach can help individuals achieve their long-term financial goals, such as buying a home, funding education, or preparing for retirement.

Understanding the different types of investments is essential for any beginner. The most common forms include stocks, bonds, and mutual funds. Stocks represent ownership in a company, allowing investors to share in its profits and losses. Bonds, on the other hand, are loans made to corporations or governments that pay interest over time. Mutual funds pool money from multiple investors to purchase a diverse range of stocks and bonds, providing a more balanced approach to investing. Each of these investment types carries its own risk and potential for return, making it important to assess your financial situation and risk tolerance before diving in.

Investing is not without its risks, and it is crucial to approach it with a strategy. One of the most effective strategies is diversification, which involves spreading investments across various asset classes to minimize risk. By not putting all your eggs in one basket, you can reduce the impact of any single investment's poor performance on your overall portfolio. Additionally, understanding market trends and economic indicators can help you make more informed decisions about when to buy or sell investments.

For beginners, starting to invest can feel overwhelming, but there are practical steps to ease the process. Setting clear financial goals is the first step; determining what you want to achieve with your investments will guide your choices. Next, consider establishing an emergency fund and paying down high-interest debt, as these steps can provide a solid financial foundation. Once you are ready to invest, consider opening a brokerage account or investing through a retirement account, such as a 401(k) or an IRA, which offer tax advantages.

In conclusion, investing is a vital skill for anyone looking to manage their finances effectively. By understanding the basic concepts of investing, the different types of investments available, and how to navigate risks, you can empower yourself to make confident financial decisions. With a strategic approach, a commitment to lifelong learning, and the willingness to adapt, investing can become a powerful tool in achieving your financial aspirations.

Different Types of Investments

Investing is a fundamental component of financial literacy and serves as a powerful tool for building wealth over time. There are various types of investments available, each with unique characteristics, risks, and potential returns. Understanding these different investment options is essential for anyone looking to grow their financial portfolio and secure their financial future. This knowledge enables individuals to make informed decisions that align with their financial goals, risk tolerance, and investment horizon.

One of the most common types of investments is stocks. When you buy stocks, you are purchasing a share of ownership in a company. Stocks can provide significant returns, especially over the long term, as companies grow and become more profitable. However, they also come with inherent risks, as stock prices can fluctuate widely based on market conditions, company performance, and economic factors. It is essential for new investors to conduct thorough research and consider diversifying their stock investments to mitigate risk while still pursuing growth opportunities.

Bonds represent another popular investment option. When you purchase a bond, you are essentially lending money to a government entity or corporation in exchange for periodic interest payments and the return of the bond's face value at maturity. Bonds are generally considered safer than stocks, making them a suitable choice for risk-averse investors or those nearing retirement. However, lower risk often corresponds to lower potential returns. Understanding the different types of bonds, such as government bonds, corporate bonds, and municipal bonds, can help investors choose the right mix for their portfolio.

Mutual funds offer a way for investors to pool their resources together to invest in a diversified portfolio managed by professionals. These funds can invest in various assets, including stocks, bonds, and other securities. Mutual funds are particularly appealing to beginner investors, as they provide instant diversification and professional management, which can help mitigate some of the risks associated with investing. It is important for investors to be aware of the fees associated with mutual funds, as these can eat into overall returns and impact investment decisions.

Real estate is another investment avenue that has gained popularity. Investing in real estate can take various forms, from purchasing rental properties to investing in real estate investment trusts (REITs). While real estate can provide a steady income stream and appreciation potential, it also requires active management and can involve significant upfront costs. Investors interested in real estate should carefully evaluate their financial situation, market conditions, and investment strategy to determine if this asset class aligns with their overall financial goals. Understanding the different types of investments available empowers individuals to create a balanced and diversified portfolio that can withstand market fluctuations and help achieve long-term financial success.

Risk and Return

Risk and return are fundamental concepts in the world of finance that every individual should understand to make informed decisions about their money. At its core, the relationship between risk and return is straightforward: higher potential returns are generally accompanied by higher risks. This principle is essential for anyone looking to invest, as it helps to shape the choices made in portfolios and savings strategies. A clear understanding of how risk affects returns can empower individuals to align their investment choices with their financial goals and risk tolerance.

When considering investments, it is crucial to recognize that not all risks are the same. Market risk, credit risk, and liquidity risk are a few types that investors should familiarize themselves with. Market risk refers to the possibility that the overall market will decline, affecting the value of investments. Credit risk involves the likelihood that a borrower may default on a loan or bond, while liquidity risk pertains to the difficulty of selling an asset without significantly affecting its price. Understanding these risks allows individuals to assess their investments more critically and choose options that align with their financial objectives and comfort levels.

The expected return is another essential aspect of this relationship. It represents the anticipated profit from an investment, taking into account potential gains and losses. Different investment vehicles, such as stocks, bonds, and mutual funds, come with varying expected returns based on their risk profiles. For example, stocks typically offer higher potential returns than bonds but also carry greater risk. By evaluating the expected return of different investments, individuals can create a balanced portfolio that aims to maximize returns while managing associated risks.

Diversification is a key strategy for managing risk while pursuing returns. By spreading investments across different asset classes, sectors, and geographic regions, individuals can reduce the impact of a poor-performing investment on their overall portfolio. This does not eliminate risk entirely but rather mitigates it by ensuring that not all investments are affected by the same market events. A diversified portfolio can provide a more stable return over time, making it an essential consideration for anyone looking to invest confidently.

Ultimately, understanding the balance of risk and return is about making informed choices that align with personal financial goals. Individuals should assess their risk tolerance, which varies from person to person and can be influenced by factors such as age, income, and financial obligations. By taking the time to analyze risk and potential returns, individuals can build a solid financial foundation, make confident investment decisions, and work toward achieving their long-term financial aspirations.

Chapter 11: Understanding Stocks, Bonds, and Mutual Funds

Introduction to Stocks

Stocks represent a fundamental concept in the world of finance and investing, serving as a pivotal point for those looking to grow their wealth and secure their financial future. At their core, stocks are shares of ownership in a company, allowing individuals to invest in businesses they believe will thrive. When you purchase a stock, you are essentially buying a piece of that company, which means you have a claim on its assets and earnings. This ownership can lead to potential profits through appreciation in stock value and dividends, making stocks an essential component of many investment portfolios.

Understanding how stocks work is crucial for anyone interested in investing. The stock market is where these transactions take place, functioning as a platform for buying and selling shares. Prices of stocks fluctuate based on various factors, including company performance, market conditions, and investor sentiment. This volatility can be daunting for beginners; however, it also presents opportunities for significant returns. It is important for new investors to educate themselves on market trends and the economic indicators that influence stock prices, as this knowledge can aid in making informed investment decisions.

Investing in stocks offers several advantages, one of which is the potential for high returns compared to other asset classes like bonds or savings accounts. Historically, the stock market has outperformed these alternatives over the long term, making it an attractive option for those looking to grow their savings. Additionally, stocks can provide income through dividends, which are payments made to shareholders from a company's profits. This can serve as a reliable income stream for investors, particularly those who are retired or seeking passive income.

However, investing in stocks also comes with risks that must be understood. The value of stocks can decline, sometimes significantly, and investors may face the possibility of losing their initial investment. It is crucial for beginners to adopt a strategy that includes diversifying their portfolio, which involves investing in a variety of stocks across different sectors and industries. This approach can help mitigate risk and provide a cushion against market downturns. Moreover, setting clear investment goals and having a long-term perspective can assist investors in navigating the ups and downs of the stock market.

In summary, stocks are an essential element of the investment landscape and can be a powerful tool for building wealth. By grasping the basics of how stocks function, their advantages, and the associated risks, individuals can confidently embark on their investing journey. As part of a broader financial toolkit, knowledge about stocks can empower beginners to make informed decisions, ultimately leading to better financial management and success in achieving their financial goals.

Introduction to Bonds

Bonds are a fundamental component of the financial markets, serving as a vital tool for both investors and issuers. At their core, bonds are essentially loans that investors provide to borrowers, typically governments or corporations. When you purchase a bond, you are lending your money in exchange for periodic interest payments, known as coupon payments, and the return of the bond's face value upon maturity. Understanding bonds is crucial for anyone looking to build a balanced investment portfolio and achieve long-term financial goals.

The bond market operates on the principle of debt financing, where entities seek to raise capital without giving up ownership stakes. Governments issue bonds to fund public projects and manage budget deficits, while corporations use them to expand operations or refinance existing debts. Each bond comes with specific terms, including its maturity date, interest rate, and credit rating, which reflects the issuer's ability to repay the borrowed funds. This intricacy makes bonds an essential topic for anyone interested in financial literacy, as they represent a safer investment avenue compared to stocks, especially for conservative investors.

Bonds are categorized into several types, each serving different purposes and appealing to various investor profiles. For instance, government bonds, such as U.S. Treasury bonds, are considered low-risk due to the government's backing. Corporate bonds, on the other hand, carry higher risks and potentially higher returns, as they depend on the financial health of the issuing company. Municipal bonds provide tax advantages and are issued by local governments to fund public projects. Understanding these distinctions helps investors make informed decisions based on their risk tolerance and investment objectives.

Interest rates play a significant role in the bond market, influencing both the performance of existing bonds and the appeal of new issues. When interest rates rise, the value of existing bonds typically falls, creating a dynamic relationship that investors must navigate. Conversely, when rates decrease, bond prices tend to rise, offering capital appreciation opportunities. For beginners in investing, grasping how interest rates affect bonds is essential for optimizing returns and managing risks in their portfolios.

Incorporating bonds into a personal investment strategy can enhance financial security and provide steady income. For individuals focusing on managing money confidently, bonds can serve as a stabilizing force in a diversified portfolio. They offer predictable cash flow and lower volatility compared to equities, making them an attractive option for risk-averse investors or those nearing retirement. By understanding the basics of bonds, individuals can take proactive steps toward financial literacy and effective money management, ultimately fostering a sense of confidence in their investment decisions.

Introduction to Mutual Funds

Mutual funds are a popular investment vehicle that allows individuals to pool their money together to invest in a diversified portfolio of stocks, bonds, and other securities. At their core, mutual funds are designed to provide investors with a way to achieve diversification and professional management without needing to select individual investments themselves. This makes them an appealing option for those who may be new to investing or those who prefer a more hands-off approach to wealth accumulation. Understanding mutual funds is a critical step in building a solid financial foundation and achieving long-term financial goals.

One of the primary benefits of investing in mutual funds is diversification. By pooling money with other investors, mutual funds can invest in a wider array of assets than most individuals could achieve on their own. This spread of investments can help reduce risk, as the performance of the fund is not solely dependent on the success of a single investment. Instead, the fund's overall risk is mitigated through its diversified portfolio. For a beginner, this means that even with a small amount of capital, they can gain exposure to a variety of sectors and industries, which can lead to more stable long-term returns.

Another appealing aspect of mutual funds is the professional management they offer. Each mutual fund is managed by a team of investment professionals who research, select, and monitor the fund's investments. This management is particularly beneficial for those who may not have the time, expertise, or interest to actively manage their investments. Fund managers utilize their knowledge of market trends and investment strategies to optimize the fund's performance, providing peace of mind for investors who may prefer to focus on other aspects of their financial journey.

While mutual funds present numerous advantages, it is essential to be aware of the costs associated with them. Investors typically pay fees, which can include management fees, performance fees, and other expenses. These fees can vary significantly between funds, and they can impact overall returns. Therefore, it is crucial for investors to carefully evaluate the fee structure of any mutual fund they consider. Understanding these costs will enable individuals to make informed decisions that align with their financial objectives and investment strategy.

In summary, mutual funds serve as an accessible entry point for beginners looking to invest. They offer diversification and professional management, making them suitable for those who may not have extensive investing knowledge or experience. However, it is vital to remain mindful of the associated costs and to conduct thorough research before committing to a particular fund. By incorporating mutual funds into a broader investment strategy, individuals can enhance their financial literacy and work towards achieving their long-term financial goals with confidence.

Chapter 12: Smart Spending

Identifying Needs vs. Wants

Identifying needs versus wants is a foundational skill in financial literacy that can significantly impact your budgeting and spending habits. Needs are essentials required for survival and basic functioning, such as food, shelter, clothing, and healthcare. In contrast, wants are non-essential items or services that enhance our lifestyle but are not necessary for basic living. Understanding this distinction is crucial as it helps prioritize your spending and ensures that your financial resources are allocated efficiently.

To effectively identify needs and wants, begin by examining your current expenses. List your monthly expenditures and categorize them into two groups: needs and wants. Needs may include rent or mortgage payments, utilities, groceries, and transportation costs. Wants might encompass dining out, entertainment subscriptions, luxury items, and travel. By clearly delineating these categories, you can visualize where your money is going and make informed decisions about your spending habits.

Recognizing the difference between needs and wants is particularly important when creating a budget. A well-structured budget prioritizes needs first, ensuring that all essential expenses are covered before allocating funds for discretionary spending. This practice not only helps in maintaining financial stability but also minimizes the risk of overspending on non-essential items. By adhering to a budget that emphasizes needs, you can create a buffer for unexpected expenses and ultimately build a more secure financial future.

Additionally, this distinction can aid in avoiding debt traps. When individuals confuse wants for needs, they may be tempted to finance non-essential purchases through credit. This can lead to accumulating debt that becomes difficult to manage. By consistently evaluating your spending through the lens of needs versus wants, you can cultivate more responsible financial habits that prioritize debt avoidance and long-term financial health.

In conclusion, mastering the ability to identify needs and wants is a critical component of financial literacy. This skill empowers individuals to take control of their financial situations by making informed choices about spending and saving. By focusing on needs first, individuals can create robust budgets, avoid unnecessary debt, and ultimately achieve their financial goals with confidence. Understanding this fundamental principle is an essential step in your journey toward effective money management and financial independence.

Strategies for Smart Shopping

Smart shopping is a vital skill in managing personal finances effectively and requires a strategic approach to ensure that every dollar spent contributes to overall financial well-being. To begin with, it is essential to set a clear budget before embarking on any shopping expedition. A well-defined budget helps prioritize needs over wants and allows individuals to allocate funds appropriately for essential expenses. By determining how much money can be spent without jeopardizing savings or essential bills, shoppers can make informed decisions and avoid impulsive purchases that may lead to financial strain.

Another effective strategy for smart shopping is to create a comprehensive shopping list. This list should be based on actual necessities, derived from careful consideration of what is truly required versus what is merely desired. By sticking to a shopping list, individuals can resist the temptation to buy items that are not needed, which often leads to overspending. Additionally, this practice encourages focus during shopping trips, making it easier to compare prices and find the best deals without getting sidetracked by attractive promotions or advertisements.

Utilizing technology can also enhance smart shopping practices. Many apps and websites allow consumers to compare prices, track spending, and even find coupons or discounts specific to their shopping needs. By leveraging these tools, shoppers can make more informed decisions that align with their budgetary constraints. Furthermore, signing up for loyalty programs with favorite retailers can yield significant savings over time, as these programs often provide exclusive discounts and rewards for frequent customers.

Timing can play a crucial role in effective shopping strategies as well. Being aware of seasonal sales, holiday discounts, and clearance events can provide opportunities to purchase items at reduced prices. Planning purchases around these times not only maximizes savings but also allows consumers to take advantage of bulk buying for items that have a longer shelf life. However, it is important to balance these opportunities with actual needs to prevent unnecessary purchases simply because an item is on sale.

Finally, cultivating a mindset of mindful consumption is essential for long-term financial health. This involves evaluating the true value of a purchase and considering its impact on personal finances and overall well-being. By asking questions such as whether an item will provide lasting satisfaction or fulfill a genuine need, shoppers can develop greater awareness of their spending habits. This reflective approach fosters responsible financial behavior, ultimately leading to more confident money management and a stronger foundation for future financial goals.

Making Informed Purchases

Making informed purchases is a fundamental aspect of sound financial management that requires both knowledge and strategy. The first step in making informed purchases is to understand your financial situation. This involves having a clear picture of your income, expenses, savings, and debt. By maintaining a detailed budget, you can identify how much discretionary income you have available for purchases. This awareness helps prevent overspending and encourages you to prioritize your needs over wants. Knowing your financial limits allows you to approach purchasing decisions with confidence and clarity.

Once you have established a budget, the next step is to conduct thorough research before making any significant purchase. This means comparing prices, reading reviews, and assessing the quality and necessity of the items you intend to buy. For example, if you're considering a major purchase such as a car or a piece of technology, take the time to explore different brands, models, and features. Online resources, consumer reports, and price comparison websites can provide valuable insights that assist in making a well-informed decision. This research not only helps you find the best deals but also ensures that you are purchasing products that provide real value.

In addition to evaluating the product itself, it is crucial to consider the payment options available. Understanding the implications of financing versus paying in cash can significantly impact your financial health. If you choose to finance a purchase, review the terms of the loan or credit agreement carefully, paying attention to interest rates and any hidden fees. Conversely, if paying cash is an option, consider the opportunity cost of using those funds. Would that money serve you better if saved or invested? Reflecting on these factors can lead to more judicious spending choices.

Moreover, the timing of your purchases can also make a difference in your financial outcomes. Seasonal sales, holiday discounts, and clearance events can provide opportunities to save money on items you need. Additionally, waiting for a short period before making a purchase can help you avoid impulse buys, giving you time to evaluate whether the item is truly necessary. This practice not only protects your budget but also fosters a mindful approach to spending that contributes to long-term financial stability.

Lastly, it is essential to cultivate a mindset that values patience and deliberation in your purchasing habits. Making informed purchases is not merely a skill but a practice that can lead to greater financial confidence over time. By integrating these strategies into your financial routine, you empower yourself to navigate the marketplace with knowledge and assurance. This proactive approach to spending not only enhances your financial literacy but also aligns your purchases with your overall financial goals, paving the way for improved money management and a more secure financial future.

Chapter 13: Practical Tips for Financial Success

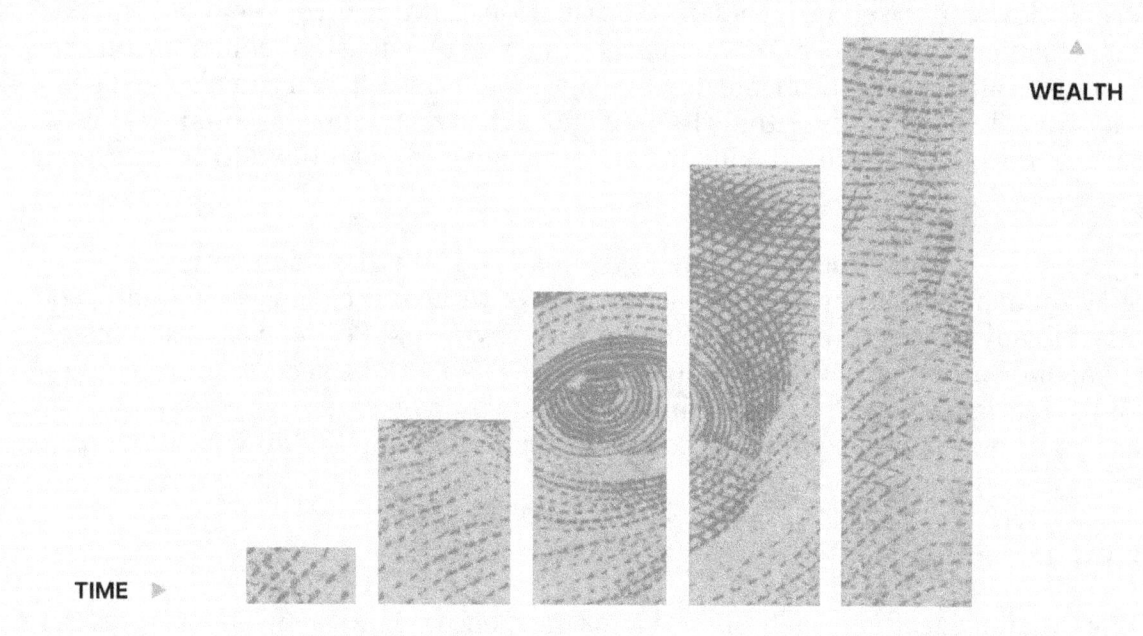

Automating Your Finances

Automating your finances is a powerful strategy that can simplify your financial management and help you stay on track with your goals. By leveraging technology, you can set up systems that handle recurring transactions, savings, and even investments on your behalf. This not only saves you time but also reduces the likelihood of human error and impulsive spending. As you embrace automation, you will find it easier to manage your budget, maintain healthy credit, and secure your financial future.

To begin automating your finances, start with your income and expenses. Most banks and financial institutions offer direct deposit options for your paycheck, ensuring that your income is automatically deposited into your checking account. From there, you can establish automatic payments for regular bills such as utilities, rent, and subscriptions. By scheduling these payments, you eliminate the risk of late fees and maintain your credit score. Additionally, consider setting up alerts for low balances or upcoming due dates to stay informed without constant monitoring.

Next, focus on your savings. Automating your savings can create a seamless pathway to your financial goals. Consider setting up a separate savings account specifically for emergencies, travel, or retirement. You can arrange for a specific amount of money to be transferred automatically from your checking account to your savings account on a regular basis, such as after each paycheck. This "pay yourself first" mentality ensures that you prioritize saving and helps you build a financial cushion without having to think about it actively.

Investing is another area where automation can be beneficial. Many investment platforms allow you to set up automatic contributions to your investment accounts. This can be particularly useful for retirement accounts, where consistent contributions can lead to significant growth over time due to compound interest. You can also explore robo-advisors, which use algorithms to manage your investments based on your risk tolerance and financial goals, making it easier than ever for beginners to get started in the market.

Finally, regularly review your automated systems to ensure they align with your changing financial situation. As your income grows, or if your expenses fluctuate, you may need to adjust your automated transfers and payments. Periodic assessments of your financial automation will help you stay on track and make necessary adjustments to avoid potential pitfalls. By automating your finances, you empower yourself to manage your money with confidence, allowing you to focus on building wealth and achieving your financial objectives.

Utilizing Financial Tools and Apps

In today's digital age, financial tools and apps have become indispensable resources for individuals seeking to manage their money more effectively. These platforms simplify budgeting, track expenses, and provide insights into spending habits. They empower users to take control of their finances by offering features that cater to various needs, from novice budgeters to seasoned investors. By integrating technology into financial management, users can cultivate a more organized and informed approach to their financial lives.

One of the primary functions of financial apps is budgeting. Many applications allow users to create personalized budgets by connecting directly to their bank accounts. This connection enables automatic tracking of income and expenses, providing a clear overview of financial health. Users can set spending limits for different categories, such as groceries, entertainment, and transportation. This feature not only fosters awareness of spending patterns but also encourages users to stick to their budgets, ultimately leading to better financial discipline.

Beyond budgeting, financial tools also play a crucial role in understanding credit and managing debt. Apps dedicated to credit monitoring give users real-time updates on their credit scores and provide insights into factors affecting their credit health. This information is vital for individuals looking to build or maintain good credit. Furthermore, some applications offer debt repayment calculators, which help users strategize their debt pay-off plans. By visualizing their progress and setting achievable goals, individuals can tackle debt with confidence, reducing the risk of falling into debt traps.

Saving for the future is another area where financial tools excel. Many apps feature automated savings options, allowing users to set aside money for emergencies, travel, or retirement effortlessly. Users can establish specific savings goals and track their progress over time, which can be highly motivating. Additionally, some platforms provide users with investment options, allowing beginners to dip their toes into the world of stocks, bonds, and mutual funds without feeling overwhelmed. These features demystify investing, making it accessible and less intimidating for those just starting.

Finally, the educational aspect of financial tools should not be overlooked. Many applications offer resources, articles, and tutorials that cover essential topics such as smart spending, building good credit, and effective saving strategies. By utilizing these resources, users can enhance their financial literacy and develop essential life skills that will serve them well in the long run. Embracing these financial tools and apps not only streamlines money management but also fosters a more confident and informed approach to personal finance, equipping individuals with the knowledge and skills needed to thrive financially.

Continuous Learning in Personal Finance

Continuous learning in personal finance is critical to developing a solid foundation for managing your money effectively. The financial landscape is ever-evolving, influenced by changes in the economy, advancements in technology, and shifts in personal circumstances. To navigate this complex environment, individuals must commit to ongoing education about budgeting basics, credit and debt management, and investment opportunities. By adopting a mindset of continuous learning, you empower yourself to make informed decisions that align with your financial goals.

One of the most effective ways to enhance your financial literacy is through actively seeking out educational resources. This can include books, online courses, podcasts, and webinars focused on various aspects of personal finance. Engaging with diverse materials expands your knowledge base and exposes you to different perspectives on money management. For instance, understanding how credit scores work and the importance of maintaining good credit can significantly impact your financial future. By continually updating your knowledge, you can adapt your strategies and make choices that best suit your evolving financial situation.

Moreover, participating in workshops or community events centered around personal finance can provide invaluable hands-on experience. These settings often encourage discussion and allow participants to share their challenges and successes. Networking with others who are also focused on improving their financial literacy can offer fresh insights and inspire new approaches to budgeting, saving, and investing. Collaboration with peers fosters an environment of accountability, where individuals can motivate each other to stay committed to their financial education journey.

Technology has also made it easier than ever to engage in continuous learning. Numerous apps and websites offer tools for tracking expenses, creating budgets, and managing investments. Many platforms provide educational content that breaks down complex concepts such as stocks, bonds, and mutual funds into digestible formats. By utilizing these digital resources, you can stay informed about market trends and new financial products, enabling you to make smart spending choices and avoid potential debt traps.

Finally, it is essential to periodically reassess your financial goals and strategies. As your circumstances change—whether due to a new job, a move, or a change in family dynamics—so too should your approach to managing your money. Regularly revisiting your budget and investment plans helps ensure that they remain aligned with your current needs and aspirations. Embracing continuous learning allows you to adapt your financial toolkit, ensuring you are equipped to address challenges and seize opportunities as they arise. By committing to lifelong financial education, you cultivate the skills necessary to manage your money with confidence and clarity.

Chapter 14: Conclusion

Recap of Essential Skills

A comprehensive understanding of essential skills in financial management is fundamental for achieving long-term financial stability and success. This recap serves as a reminder of the core competencies covered in this book, enabling readers to apply these concepts confidently in their everyday lives. First and foremost, mastering the basics of managing money involves developing a clear budget. A budget is more than just a list of income and expenses; it reflects your financial goals, helps track spending habits, and facilitates informed decision-making. Utilizing step-by-step budget templates can simplify this process, allowing individuals to visualize their financial situation and adjust their habits accordingly.

Understanding credit and debt is another vital skill that can significantly impact one's financial health. Knowledge of credit scores, the factors that influence them, and the importance of maintaining good credit can empower individuals to make smarter borrowing choices. Learning how to avoid common debt traps, such as high-interest loans or credit card pitfalls, is crucial. By cultivating good credit habits, such as timely payments and responsible credit utilization, individuals can improve their financial profiles and access better lending options when needed.

Saving for the future is equally essential in building a robust financial foundation. Establishing an emergency fund is a fundamental step, serving as a safety net in times of unexpected expenses. Additionally, understanding the various saving vehicles available, such as high-yield savings accounts and retirement accounts, can help individuals maximize their savings potential. The emphasis on setting specific savings goals, whether for a vacation, a major purchase, or retirement, encourages a proactive approach to financial planning.

Investing can seem daunting for beginners, yet it is a critical skill that can lead to wealth accumulation over time. A basic grasp of investment concepts, including stocks, bonds, and mutual funds, allows individuals to make informed choices about where to allocate their money. Recognizing the difference between these investment options and understanding risk versus reward can empower readers to create a diversified portfolio that aligns with their financial goals. Moreover, learning about the importance of starting early and the benefits of compound interest can motivate individuals to prioritize investing as part of their financial strategy.

Lastly, smart spending is a skill that should not be overlooked. This involves making conscious choices about purchases and seeking value in every transaction. Techniques such as comparison shopping, leveraging discounts, and prioritizing needs over wants can lead to significant savings. By implementing practical tips and strategies learned throughout this book, individuals can transform their financial habits, leading to a more confident and secure financial future. Recapping these essential skills reinforces the importance of financial literacy as a lifelong journey, equipping readers to navigate the complexities of money management with confidence.

Your Financial Journey Ahead

Your financial journey ahead is an important chapter in mastering the art of money management. It begins with a clear understanding of where you currently stand financially, which is essential for setting realistic goals. Take stock of your income, expenses, assets, and liabilities. This self-assessment will not only highlight your financial strengths but also reveal areas that require improvement. By establishing a baseline, you can create a roadmap that guides your spending, saving, and investing decisions effectively.

As you map out your financial journey, budgeting will become one of your most valuable tools. A well-structured budget allows you to allocate resources wisely, ensuring that your essential needs are met while also allowing room for savings and discretionary spending. Start by categorizing your expenses into fixed and variable costs. Use step-by-step budget templates to create a plan that reflects your income and spending habits. This process will empower you to take control of your finances, making informed decisions that align with your goals.

Understanding credit and debt is another crucial component of your financial journey. Good credit can open doors to better loan terms and lower interest rates, while poor credit can hinder your financial progress. Educate yourself on how credit scores are calculated, and take proactive steps to build and maintain strong credit. Pay your bills on time, keep credit utilization low, and regularly check your credit reports for inaccuracies. By prioritizing good credit management, you will enhance your financial opportunities for years to come.

Saving for the future should be a non-negotiable aspect of your financial journey. Establishing an emergency fund is the first step, providing you with a safety net for unexpected expenses. Aim to save three to six months' worth of living expenses in a separate savings account. From there, consider other savings goals, such as retirement or major purchases. Automating your savings can help you stay consistent, making it easier to reach your financial milestones without overthinking each transaction.

Finally, as you venture into the world of investing, it is essential to approach it with a clear understanding of your risk tolerance and investment goals. Familiarize yourself with fundamental concepts like stocks, bonds, and mutual funds. Start small, diversifying your investments to mitigate risk while seeking growth opportunities. Remember that investing is a long-term endeavor, and patience is key. By educating yourself and making informed decisions, you will not only enhance your financial literacy but also build a solid foundation for a prosperous future.

Here's a list of suggested resources including books, websites, and apps that will deepen your understanding and some practical tools.

Financial Literacy 101: Managing Money with Confidence

- Books:
- I Will Teach You to Be Rich by Ramit Sethi
- Your Money or Your Life by Vicki Robin and Joe Dominguez
- Websites:
- Investopedia (www.investopedia.com) for investment basics
- NerdWallet (www.nerdwallet.com) for comparisons on banking, credit cards, and loans
- Apps:
- Mint (for budgeting)
- Acorns or Robinhood (for beginner-friendly investing)

Dear Reader,

As you finish this guide, remember that financial skills develop over time, with each new experience adding to your knowledge. Don't be discouraged by setbacks; they're simply part of the learning journey. Every step you take to manage your money brings you closer to financial security and freedom. You have everything you need to build a stable future—one decision at a time. Keep going, stay curious, and trust yourself. You've got this!

Warm regards,

Monica Lynne Chase